# BMX Bicycles

By E. S. Budd

The Child's World®

Published by The Child's World®
PO Box 326
Chanhassen, MN 55317-0326
800-599-READ
www.childsworld.com

Design and Production:
The Creative Spark, San Juan Capistrano, CA

Photo Credits: Images ©2004 David M. Budd Photography.

**Library of Congress Cataloging-in-Publication Data**
Budd, E. S.
 BMX bicycles / by E.S. Budd.
    p. cm. — (Machines at work)
 ISBN 1-59296-161-4 (Library bound : alk. paper)
 1.  BMX bikes—Juvenile literature. [1. BMX bikes. 2. Bicycle motocross.]  I. Title.
TL437.5.B58B84 2004
629.227'2—dc22
                                    2003023663

# Contents

# Let's Try BMX!

BMX stands for bicycle **motocross.**
It's an exciting sport! Girls and boys,
kids and adults—anyone can do it.
BMX riders are called BMXers. They
race on dirt tracks at high speeds. They
enjoy doing tricks and jumps. People
all over the world participate in BMX.

The first BMXers were kids who wanted to try motocross. Most were too young to ride motorcycles. So they thought they'd try doing the sport on their bicycles. They built tracks with bumps, hills, and sharp turns—just like those used for motocross. Then they began to organize races.

Before they knew it, the kids had created a whole new sport—bicycle motocross. Then the American Bicycle Association was founded to organize races. It created a set of rules for BMX racing.

So how do you get started in BMX? The first thing you need is a bike! Make sure the **frame** is the right size for you. Never use a bike that's too big or too small. Most BMX bikes should have 20-inch wheels. Some have 24-inch wheels. They are called cruisers.

A BMX bicycle must have three safety pads. One pad is on the top tube of the frame. Another pad wraps around the **stem.** The third pad is on the **crossbar.**

BMX bikes do not have a kickstand or a **chainguard.** They also do not have reflectors. In an accident, all of these parts can cause injuries. For safety, these bike parts are removed.

BMX is an extreme sport. That means it's fast, exciting—and sometimes dangerous. But BMX doesn't have to be risky. In fact, it's no more dangerous than football, soccer, and other common sports.

In BMX, it's important to stay in control, have the right gear, and ride a safe bicycle. Officials inspect all bikes before a BMX race. They make sure the bikes are working well.

So what gear do you need to ride a BMX bicycle? First, you need long pants and a long-sleeved shirt. These clothes protect riders when they fall. Riders who compete in races often wear a BMX uniform. It includes a shirt and racing pants made of heavy material. They have special padding for even more protection. Many BMXers also wear gloves to protect their hands. Sturdy shoes or boots are important, too.

It's always a good idea to wear a helmet whenever you ride a bike. You should never race BMX without one.

Are you ready to race? BMXers participate in a series of races called **motos.** They race against other riders in the same age group. When it's time, riders in a moto line up at the starting gate.

The gate drops, and it's time to start pedaling!

In one day, racers usually ride in three or four motos. These races are short and last about 35 to 45 seconds. Winners of the motos go on to the finals at the end of the day.

Remember that BMX takes practice. It may take some time to win your first race. But you'll soon take home trophies. Once you get the hang of it, you can do BMX for many years to come.

There's more to BMX than just racing.
Some people enjoy freestyle BMX, or
stunt riding. They do tricks and jumps,
catching air and having fun.

# Climb Aboard!

Would you like to see what it's like to ride a BMX bicycle? You'll need protective clothing. You can wear a long-sleeved shirt and a pair of jeans. Later, you may want to buy a BMX uniform. Don't forget your helmet!

# Up Close

BMX bicycles have 20- or 24-inch wheels with knobby tires. These special tires create **traction.** The **fork** attaches the front wheel to the handlebars. The handlebars are used to steer the bike. A hand **brake** helps riders control their speed. BMX bikes have special pads to protect riders.

1. Frame

2. Wheels

3. Fork

4. Handlebars

5. Frame pad

6. Crossbar pad

7. Stem pad

8. Hand brake

# Glossary

**brake (BRAYK)** A brake is a control that helps a rider stop or slow down. A BMX bike has a hand brake.

**chainguard (CHAYN-gard)** A chainguard is a part on a bicycle that covers the chain. A BMX bike does not have a chainguard.

**crossbar (KROSS-bar)** A crossbar is a metal bar that connects the two ends of the handlebars. A BMX bike has a pad on the crossbar.

**fork (FORK)** A fork attaches the front wheel of a bicycle to the handlebars. A BMX bike has a fork made of sturdy metal.

**frame (FRAYM)** A frame is the skeleton of a bicycle. A BMX bike has a frame made of sturdy metal.

**motocross (MOH-toh-cross)** Motocross is a sport in which motorcycles are raced on a dirt course with sharp turns and jumps. The first BMX riders copied motocross using bicycles instead of motorcycles.

**motos (MOH-tohz)** Motos are races at a BMX event. The winner of a series of motos goes on to race in the finals.

**stem (STEM)** A stem connects the handlebars to the fork on a bicycle. A BMX bike has a pad on the stem.

**traction (TRAK-shun)** Traction is friction that helps to move a vehicle forward and keep it from sliding. Knobby tires on a BMX bike provide traction.